CONTENTS

D0111496

Cal Ripken, Jr., connects for a home-run blast!

CAL
RIPKEN, JR.

HALL OF FAME
BASEBALL SUPERSTAR

**Glen
Macnow**

Shooting Star

Library of Congress Cataloging-in-Publication Data

Macnow, Glen.

    Cal Ripken, Jr. : Hall of Fame baseball superstar / Glen Macnow.

      p. cm. — (Hall of fame sports greats)

    Rev. ed. of: Sports great Cal Ripken, Jr.

    Includes bibliographical references and index.

    Summary: "Read about Hall of Fame baseball player, Cal Ripken, Jr., in this sports biography. Learn about the Iron Man, and how he became the legendary player that he is"—Provided by publisher.

    ISBN 978-1-62285-020-4 (alk. paper)

    1. Ripken, Cal, 1960- —Juvenile literature. 2. Baseball players—United States—Biography—Juvenile literature. I. Macnow, Glen. Sports great Cal Ripken, Jr. II. Title.

    GV865.R47M32 2013

    796.357092—dc23

    [B]   2012044915

Paperback ISBN: 978-1-62285-021-1   EPUB ISBN: 978-1-62285-023-5
Single-User ISBN: 978-1-62285-024-2   Multi-User PDF: 978-1-62285-147-8

Printed in the United States of America
052013 Lake Book Manufacturing, Inc., Melrose Park, IL
10 9 8 7 6 5 4 3 2 1

To Our Readers: We have done our best to make sure all Internet addresses in this book were active and appropriate when we went to press. However, the author and the Publisher have no control over, and assume no liability for, the material available on those Internet sites or on other Web sites they may link to. Any comments or suggestions can be sent by e-mail to comments@speedingstar.com or to the address below:

Speeding Star
Box 398, 40 Industrial Road
Berkeley Heights, NJ 07922
USA
www.speedingstar.com

Photo Credits: AP Images, pp. 11, 30; AP Images/Bill Kostroun, p. 9; AP Images/Dave Hammond, p. 39; AP Images/Denis Paquin, pp. 17, 55; AP Images/Eugene Hoshiko, p. 29; AP Images/Gail Burton, p. 36; AP Images/Harry Harris, p. 14; AP Images/Joe Skipper, p. 33; AP Images/John Swart, p. 20; AP Images/Linda Kaye, p. 42; AP Images/Mark J. Terrill, p. 57; AP Images/Mark Lennihan, pp. 1, 51; AP Images/Mike Groll, p. 59; AP Images/Nick Wass, p. 26; AP Images/Roberto Borea, pp. 4, 47.

Cover Illustration: AP Images/Mark Lennihan

This title was originally published in 1993 as *Sports Great Cal Ripken, Jr.*

The Perfect Baseball Player

Imagine if you could build the perfect baseball player. What would he be like?

First, he would be strong. He would play every day, even if he had the flu or a sprained ankle. He would never ask to rest during the second game of a doubleheader. He would never want to be taken out for a pinch hitter against a tough pitcher like Nolan Ryan.

Second, he would be a shortstop, because that is perhaps the toughest position to play. He would be among the best fielders, bobbling few grounders and gracefully turning the double play. His arm would be strong and true.

Third, he would be a great hitter. Each season his team could count on him for 25 home runs, 35 doubles, and 100 runs batted in. He would play even better when the game was on the line. As he got older, his stroke would become even more powerful.

You could add other qualities to this fantasy ballplayer. Make him loyal, the type who would play forever in one city and never try to leave for more money. Make him polite to fans and reporters. Make him a leader among teammates and liked even by opponents. Make him Rookie of the Year and a two-time Most Valuable Player.

Want to go further? Imagine that this player is the son of a coach and the big brother of the second baseman. That would be the perfect player. He would even be wholesome enough to do commercials for milk. Of course, such a player seems too perfect to ever be real. But he is.

Cal Ripken, Jr., is all those things. He was an all-star shortstop for the Baltimore Orioles. He was both a great hitter and a great fielder. He was durable enough to break Lou Gehrig's record of 2,130 consecutive games on September 6, 1995. In 1996 he broke the world's longest consecutive game streak of 2,215. He would carry both records out to 2,632 consecutive games before giving himself the day off on September 20, 1996.

Ripken played on a team where his brother Billy was the second baseman. His father, Cal, Sr., once managed the club and was also the third-base coach. "When we were boys, Billy and I would pretend we were grown-ups playing together in the major leagues," Cal says. "I think all brothers pretend that way. But in our case, the dream came true."

In many ways, Ripken is a baseball fan's dream come true. At six foot four and 220 pounds, he remains the biggest shortstop in major-league history. Still, his defense was so steady that he would be considered a star player even if he hit just .240 every year.

In 1990, for example, Cal set a major-league record by making just three errors in a whole season. How good is that? Consider that Brooks Robinson, widely considered the best-fielding third baseman ever, once made three errors in one inning. Robinson was Cal's hero as a child.

As good as Ripken's fielding was, his hitting was even better. He was the first shortstop ever to hit 20 or more home runs in 10 straight seasons. In 1991, the year in which he won his second Most Valuable Player (MVP) award, Cal piled up a .323 batting average, 46 doubles, 34 homers, and 114 runs batted in (RBIs).

"I never saw some of the old-timers," once said Hall of Fame manager Sparky Anderson." "But in all my fifty-seven years, Ripken is the best shortstop I've ever seen. He's the complete package."

Is Ripken the top shortstop ever? That's difficult to say. Baseball historians usually regard Honus Wagner as the best. Wagner played twenty-one seasons, mostly for the Pittsburgh Pirates. He was a fluid fielder, and his .329 lifetime batting average is among the highest ever. But Wagner's career ended in 1917. Few alive today ever saw him play and can compare him to Ripken.

Later, Ernie Banks of the Chicago Cubs was called the best. Banks played from 1953 to 1971. He twice led the National

League in home runs. Like Cal, he was twice named the Most Valuable Player. But after nine seasons at shortstop, he was moved to first base and sometimes played third base or the outfield.

Three shortstops emerged in the 1990s that many thought could become the best ever. Nomar Garciaparra of the Red Sox had seven great seasons as a shortstop, but injuries cut his career a bit short. For ten years, Alex Rodriguez was considered the best hitting shortstop of all-time. But when he signed with the New York Yankees he switched to third base. That leaves Rodriguez's teammate, Derek Jeter. By the end of the 2012 baseball season, Jeter had amassed 3,304 hits, eleventh on the all-time list. A very good fielder, Jeter has won 5 Gold Glove Awards. He is also considered to be among the best postseason players in baseball history. Yet he cannot match Ripken's power numbers.

So, it can be argued that Ripken was the top shortstop of the past fifty years. But no shortstop or third baseman comes close to his record of starting in 16 straight All-Star games.

Despite it all, Ripken got noticed much less than most major-league superstars. Others make headlines for complaining about their contracts or abusing drugs or arguing with umpires. But Cal only drew notice for his good play. And playing in Baltimore, he did not get the attention he would in a larger city such as New York or Los Angeles or Chicago.

For one week in 1991, however, Ripken took baseball's center stage. As usual, Cal was voted by fans to be the American League (AL)'s starting shortstop in the All-Star game. He came to the game, in Toronto, leading the league in batting and second in home runs.

The day before the All-Star game, some of baseball's top sluggers gathered at the Toronto SkyDome for a homer-hitting contest. Will Clark of the San Francisco Giants was there. So was Howard Johnson of the New York Mets. Many thought that Darryl Strawberry of the Los Angeles Dodgers would win

Ripken was an elite hitter, and baseball's most durable player. But he also excelled in the field, winning two Gold Glove Awards as the best fielding shortstop in the American League.

the Home Run Derby. Another favorite was Cecil Fielder, the gigantic belter for the Detroit Tigers.

In all, there were eight players in the contest, including Cal. The seven other men took 85 swings against batting-practice pitching. They combined for 15 homers.

Ripken took 22 swings. He hit an astonishing 12 homers, some of them way into the upper deck.

One of Cal's blasts nearly hit a hot-dog vendor in the stands 440 feet away. Almost before that ball landed, another shot went 450 feet into the third deck. On his last swing, Ripken decided to dig down deep. He hit the longest ball of his life. It was a 475-foot belt that might have gone farther had a brave fan not reached up to stop it. The ball fell in the fifth deck at the SkyDome. Only Jose Canseco had reached that deck before.

The other players could hardly believe Cal's performance. "I've never done anything close to that," said Chicago White Sox catcher Carlton Fisk. "In fact, I've never seen another player do anything like that."

Ripken continued his super performance during the All-Star game the next night. In the first inning, he whacked a single off of Tom Glavine, the National League's starting pitcher. Then, in the third, he came up against Dennis Martinez, the tough curveball specialist.

American League stars Rickey Henderson and Wade Boggs were already on base when Ripken came to bat. Martinez threw two low pitches for balls, then a called strike. On the next pitch, he hung a slider, and Ripken jumped at it. The ball exploded off of Cal's bat. It sailed over the left-field wall as 52,000 fans cheered.

Ripken's home run gave his side a 3-1 lead. The AL went on to win, 4-2. Cal was chosen as the game's Most Valuable Player.

Late in the game, Ripken was due to bat against Rob Dibble, the Cincinnati Reds hard-throwing relief pitcher. But AL manager Tony LaRussa said he wanted to give each all-star a chance to play. So he sent Ozzie Guillen up to pinch-hit for Ripken.

Cal made it clear that he would have liked to stay in the game. But he did not complain.

"Dibble throws the ball a hundred miles an

In addition to having been a Hall-of-Fame baseball player, Cal Ripken, Jr., has become a true legend of the game.

hour," Ripken said. "I was looking forward to the challenge. But I understand that Ozzie is here to play, too. I had no problem sitting down."

Other players might have complained about being pulled after hitting a home run, but not Cal. In his mind, there is nothing to be gained by moaning. He always tries to lead by example, both on and off the field.

That, he explains, comes easily. After all, it is the way he was brought up.

Chapter

2

Bird in
the Nest

Many boys learn how to hit a baseball by batting against their fathers. Cal Ripken, Jr., was no different. Except that young Cal did not take his swings in the backyard or at a local park. He took them at real baseball stadiums all across the country.

Cal's dad, Cal Ripken, Sr., started out as a minor-league catcher for the Baltimore Orioles. But in 1960, the year Cal was born, Mr. Ripken hurt his shoulder. He could no longer throw well. So the club offered him a job as a minor-league manager.

For the next fifteen years, Mr. Ripken moved from town to town while working for the Orioles. There were eighteen stops in all: from Leesburg, Florida, to Appleton, Wisconsin,

Cal Ripken, Jr., learned about hard work and baseball from watching his dad, Cal Ripken, Sr.

to Elmira, New York, to Dallas, Texas. During the school year, young Cal, his brothers and sister, and his mom stayed at their home in Aberdeen, Maryland. But when the summer started, they loaded up a trailer and moved to wherever Mr. Ripken was managing.

The travel was both fun and tough for the Ripken kids. They had to leave their friends behind each summer and make new friends. Mostly, they were pals with one another. Cal, the oldest, recalls how he used to fight with his brothers Fred and Billy, and his sister Ellen. But they would make up and invent games by the hour. Baseball was always the biggest part of their lives. They talked about it at the dinner table and on long car rides. Even the bedtime stories Mr. Ripken told his children usually had to do with baseball.

The best part for Cal was watching his dad teach young players. Even as a little boy, he thirsted for a locker of his own. He spent summers hanging around the locker room, wearing a miniature Orioles uniform, and getting baseball tips from all the players. Years later, when he became a superstar, Cal realized how well that time had paid off. He said, "I got to learn the game from people who really knew it. Most kids don't get the chance to watch real players every day."

Sometimes Mr. Ripken would take Cal and his brothers onto the field for batting practice. Even when Cal was young, his dad would throw curveballs and fastballs, knuckleballs, and sliders. Cal was soon able to hit each pitch. At twelve, he hit his first ball out of the park. At thirteen, he put on his dad's big catcher's mitt and started catching 80-mile-per-hour fastballs from minor-league pitchers.

Mr. Ripken did not want to push his sons into playing baseball. It was his job and he loved it, he explained. But he wanted the boys to do whatever they enjoyed. Fred, the middle brother, gave up the sport at age nine because he did not like practicing. But Cal and Billy loved it. They couldn't get enough. Cal later described it as a kind of hunger that he always needed to feed.

As much as Mr. Ripken wanted to help, his job kept him too busy to spend a lot of time coaching his sons. So Cal's mom, Violet Ripken, took over. She knew baseball from all her years with Cal's dad. She knew when Cal's batting stance was out of whack or when he was holding his glove wrong in the field. Years later, Cal would remember a Little League game he pitched when he was eleven. It was 30 degrees, and the wind was so strong that he was blown off the mound. The stands were empty except for one woman with an Orioles cap pulled down over her ears. It was his mom.

When Cal was fifteen, his dad became a coach with the big-league Orioles in Baltimore. Cal had a chance to see the sport's greatest players up close. He used to sit around the team's clubhouse and listen to men like Al Bumbry, Bobby Grich, and Doug DeCinces talk about details of the game. He took pitching lessons from Hall of Famer Jim Palmer.

On weekends, Cal and Billy would come early to Baltimore's Memorial Stadium. They would shag flies in the outfield, take batting practice from real major-league pitchers, and work as

Ripken's parents, Violet and Cal, Sr., were in attendance when he broke Lou Gehrig's record for consecutive games played. Ripken, Jr., credits the support of both his mom and dad for making him the player and person he is today.

batboys during the game. On week nights, Cal would arrive at the ballpark around the fifth inning, after playing in his own high school game. In fact, he would still be wearing his dirty uniform. The stadium ticket-takers knew who he was and let him in for free.

These days Ripken is famous as a Hall-of-Fame shortstop and third baseman. But he first was noticed by pro scouts as a pitcher. Cal liked pitching best because it put him in the middle of the action and in control of every play. At Aberdeen High School outside of Baltimore, he was the school's star hurler. All those private lessons from Palmer were paying off. Cal's fastball was not great, but he almost never walked batters. As a high school senior, he won seven games, lost just two, and allowed less than one run a game.

In games he wasn't pitching, Cal played shortstop. In his last year of high school, he batted .492 with 29 RBIs in just 20 games.

The major-league scouts began coming to watch his games. Many thought that he could make it to the majors as either a pitcher or a shortstop. Several clubs said they were interested in drafting him. Cal, of course, hoped he would end up with the Orioles. And why wouldn't he? He had grown up around the team. His friends were there. So was his father.

Cal got his wish. The Orioles picked him in the second round of the 1978 draft. There was just one question left: What position would he play? Cal and the club's coaches agreed that he would be more valuable playing every day, rather than pitching once every five days. From that point on, he played only in the infield.

That summer, at age seventeen, Cal went to play for the Bluefield Orioles of the Appalachian Rookie League. Living away from home was a tough adjustment. But Cal had prepared his whole life for pro ball. He was ready. In 63 games he batted just .264 and was too skinny to hit any homers, but he was chosen as the league's best fielder by its managers.

The next season, Cal was promoted to Single-A Miami and then Double-A Charlotte. He began to bulk up, and his hitting improved. In 1980 he played the whole year at Charlotte. He smashed 25 homers and was named to the Southern League's All-Star team.

Ripken started the 1981 season at Triple-A Rochester, one step away from the major leagues. He dominated the league's pitchers so much that the Orioles could no longer keep him down in the farm system. That September, they called him up to the big leagues.

Until then everything had come easy for Ripken. But major-league pitchers threw a little bit harder than what he was used to. Major-league fielders got to some of his balls that would have fallen through for hits in the minors. In 23 games with the Orioles that fall, Cal batted just .128 with no home runs.

Cal began to worry about whether he was good enough to make it. Years later he said, "There's always a point where you question if you can do it in the majors, even if you've done it in the minors. I was beginning to wonder whether the Orioles would stick with me." Rather than just worry, Cal spent that

Ripken finished the 1982 season strong and was named AL Rookie of the Year. He is shown here lacing a hit in 1983, the year that he would become one of the league's elite players.

off-season working harder than ever. He lifted weights to improve his strength. He took batting practice every day. And he asked his father for help. In this case, the talk wasn't father to son; it was coach to player. Before the 1982 season, the Orioles traded third baseman Doug DeCinces. They told Cal he would shift back and forth between shortstop and third base. Cal said he was ready.

But he wasn't. Through the first 25 games, he was hitting just .117. Some fans and writers began to say that he was on the club only because his father was a coach. And the more that manager Earl Weaver kept telling Cal that things would improve, the more the twenty-one year old began to worry he would be a permanent flop. Then, during a game in May, Reggie Jackson of the California Angels pulled Ripken aside during a break in the action. Jackson was a superstar who had gone through tough times early in his career. He had some advice.

"Hey, kid," Jackson said. "You're pressing too hard. Don't try to be Babe Ruth. Just be yourself. Do what Cal Ripken can do."

The words clicked in Cal's mind. They jolted him into realizing that he had been putting too much pressure on himself to become an immediate star. The next day, feeling more relaxed at the plate, he got two hits. From the dugout, Jackson gave him the thumbs-up sign. The day after that, Cal had two more hits.

From that point on, Ripken was unstoppable. At season's end, he led all first-year players with 28 homers and 93 RBIs. He raised his batting average to .264, a long way from what it had been in early May. And he played in 160 of the club's 162 games, an early sign of his toughness.

The newspaper writers who cover the American League rewarded Cal by voting him Rookie of the Year, ahead of Kent Hrbek of the Minnesota Twins and Wade Boggs of the Boston Red Sox. Ripken, as usual, was modest when he got the award. "My manager and my teammates really deserve it," he said. "They stuck with me when I wasn't doing the job."

Now, he said, the goal was to get the Orioles to a World Series.

Chapter 3

Superstar

During a great athlete's career, the time usually comes when fans suddenly say: "This is a superstar." It might occur when the player leads his team to a championship. Or it might come during a season in which the player proves that he is among the best in his sport.

For Cal Ripken, the moment came in 1983. At the young age of twenty-three, Cal led the Orioles to a World Series victory. He was also chosen the AL's Most Valuable Player for batting .318 and leading the league in doubles, runs, and hits. And he played in every inning of every game, starting an amazing streak that would run for many seasons.

Suddenly, people began to realize that Cal wasn't just a promising young ballplayer. He was the best in the business.

"I don't think I've ever seen a player who was so good at such a young age," said Brooks Robinson, the Hall-of-Fame third baseman. Robinson said he was glad that the Orioles finally decided to keep Ripken at shortstop because "I didn't want to be known as the second-best third baseman the Orioles ever had."

Ripken's 1983 season was so good that it seemed to be make-believe. In just his first full season at shortstop, he quickly became the league's top fielder. He learned to move quickly to his left and his right, to charge slow-hit grounders, and to turn the double play. His powerful throws seemed like they came from a rocket launcher.

Because he is so tall, Cal was not as flashy as many shortstops who played the game. His dives and twirls rarely made the highlight films. But he was a smart player. He always seemed to be right where the ball was hit, and the reason had nothing to do with luck. It came from years of studying where each batter was likely to hit the ball. That allowed Cal to position himself in the right spot.

Ripken's size helped him in other areas. Most shortstops are slap hitters. They rarely rank among the top hitters. They almost never belt home runs. But Cal, because of his strength, quickly became one of the American League's most-feared sluggers. He smacked 27 homers in 1983. In fact, Cal hit more than 20 home runs in each of his first ten seasons.

"The way to hit home runs," Ripken once said, "is not to try to hit them. In other words, if you aim for a homer, chances are you'll fall short. But if you just try to hit the ball, the home runs will follow."

The 1983 Orioles were one of the best teams of the decade. Their strength was their pitching staff, which featured Scott McGregor, Storm Davis, Mike Boddicker, and Dennis Martinez. There were two star batters: Cal and first baseman Eddie Murray. In fact, Murray finished right behind Ripken in the MVP voting. He and Cal were best friends on the team.

The Orioles won 98 games that season to take the AL East. They had no problem whipping the Chicago White Sox in the playoffs, winning that series three games to one. Cal batted .400 for the series, scoring five runs and driving in two. He was in a groove. Every ball off his bat seemed to fall for a hit. Every time he jumped, the ball ended up in his glove. The game, he told an interviewer after the playoffs, seemed easy.

In the World Series, however, things quickly got more difficult. The Orioles faced the National League champion Philadelphia Phillies, who had star pitchers Steve Carlton and John Denny. Cal's bat suddenly got cold. He managed just three singles in 18 at bats during the series. He had no doubles, no homers, and just one RBI. His fielding continued to be great. But Cal worried that he was letting down his teammates.

He wasn't. As tough as the Phillies' pitchers were, the Orioles' pitchers were better. In five games, they allowed the Phils to score just nine runs. The Orioles won the World Series four games to one. Now Cal was a Most Valuable Player and a member of the championship team. He and his teammates celebrated by driving in a ticker-tape parade through downtown Baltimore. Things don't get much better than that.

Cal won other awards after the 1983 season. He seemed the favorite of every group voting for a player of the year. There were two reasons. First, of course, was his outstanding performance on the field. Second, was the way Cal handled himself off the field. Unlike some players, he loved being a

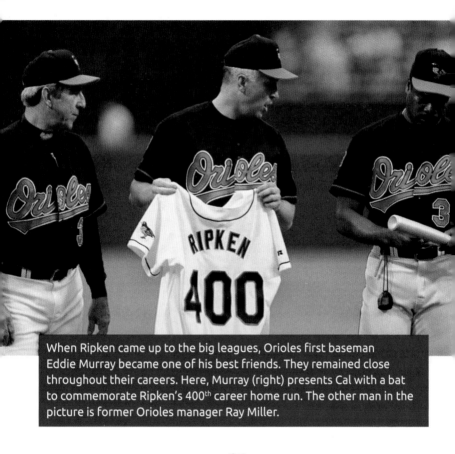

When Ripken came up to the big leagues, Orioles first baseman Eddie Murray became one of his best friends. They remained close throughout their careers. Here, Murray (right) presents Cal with a bat to commemorate Ripken's 400th career home run. The other man in the picture is former Orioles manager Ray Miller.

role model for children. So he tries to be the best person he can in order to set a good example.

"Kids look up to athletes," he said. "I know I did when I was young. If a kid playing ball in the backyard wants to pretend to be Cal Ripken, Jr., when he's swinging the bat, I want to be a good role model for him. I don't want to do anything wrong to ruin that image."

To set a good example, Cal helped set up a program called "Don't Start Smoking." Its aim was to convince teenagers to stay off cigarettes. He has been active in many charities in Baltimore. And he gives speeches warning children to keep away from drugs. "I've never had the urge to try drugs," he said, "because I believe they can harm your body."

In fact, Ripken took such good care of himself that teammates said that they never even saw him eat a candy bar. He practiced and exercised as hard as anyone on the Orioles. His body was 225 pounds of pure muscle. That dedication to hard work helped Cal stay at the top of his game.

Many athletes are unable to remain stars for a long time. Sometimes their opponents adjust and catch up with them. Other times, they get fat and lazy from too much success. They lose the ambition that made them stars in the first place.

But Ripken was too talented to be stopped by the other team. And he was too devoted to start giving anything less than his best effort. Even as a rookie, he used to say that his goal was to have a long career, and play in the majors for at least fifteen years. No one does that without always giving 100 percent.

That dedication showed in 1984. Many fans wondered

whether Ripken's MVP season would be a fluke. Would he be able to follow it up with another solid year? Their doubts were quickly removed. He came back to hit .304 and again hit 27 home runs. He also set an American League record for assists by a shortstop by throwing out 583 base runners. The year turned out to be as good as the last one.

In fact, every season during the first part of Ripken's career seemed almost identical. Look at his season-by-season home run marks for six years starting in 1982: 28, 27, 27, 26, 25, 27. That's as consistent as a player can get. From 1983 through 1986, he averaged .296 with 109 runs scored and 95 RBIs.

Plus, Cal played not just in every game. He played every inning of every game. From June 5, 1982, until September 14, 1987, Ripken never sat down for a pinch hitter or defensive replacement. He totaled 8,243 innings in a row. That is a major-league record that no one ever figures to challenge.

His toughness shows not just in durability, but also in Ripken's approach to baseball. One time, in 1983, White Sox pitcher Rich Dotson wanted to get Ripken to stop crowding home plate. Dotson threw an inside fastball that drilled Cal in the ribs. Cal refused to show that he was hurt by rubbing the bruise. And when he got to first base, he shouted at Dotson, "Is that as hard as you can throw?" The next time he faced Dotson, Ripken got even in another way. He slammed a double.

By the mid-1980s, there were no more debates on who was baseball's best shortstop. It was the tall home-run hitter from Baltimore. Other shortstops had great seasons, like Ozzie Smith of the St. Louis Cardinals, Alan Trammell of the Detroit Tigers, and Tony Fernandez of the Toronto Blue Jays. But Ripken had a great season every single year. Baseball's fans recognized this achievement. For 13 seasons in a row, starting in 1984, they voted Cal the starting AL shortstop in the All-Star game. He also started the next three All-Star games at third base, which gave him a streak of 16 consecutive starts in the All-Star game.

As steady as Ripken was, the Orioles were getting worse

Ripken takes being a role model very seriously. He is shown here conducting a baseball clinic for young people in China.

The Orioles promoted Cal, Sr., to manage the team in 1987.

around him. After winning the World Series in 1983, they slipped to 85 wins in 1984, then to 83 in 1985. In 1986, Baltimore had its first losing season in nineteen years, winning just 73 games and losing 89. Clearly, changes had to be made.

The first change was the manager. Earl Weaver, who had led the Orioles for seventeen seasons, decided to retire. Weaver was one of the all-time greats. Replacing him would not be easy. But the Orioles had a good candidate whom they had already prepared to take the job. He had spent many seasons as the third-base coach. His name was Cal Ripken, Sr., Cal's dad.

Baltimore also needed to change some of its players. A few had gotten old and were no longer very good. A few others did not turn out to be as talented as the Orioles had expected. So the club made a lot of trades heading into the 1987 season. One position they did not trade for, of course, was shortstop. Another was second base. The Orioles needed a new player at second. But they thought they had a good one ready to come up from their minor-league team. His name was Billy Ripken, Cal's brother.

"I don't know how well we will do next season," Cal told reporters after his father was hired to manage the club. "But I'll tell you one thing. It's sure going to be interesting."

Chapter 4

A Family Affair

Remember how Mr. Ripken had pitched batting practice to his sons when they were growing up? At the time, Cal and Billy liked to pretend that they were teammates in the big leagues. Of course, they figured it was just a dream.

But the dream came true in 1987. When Mr. Ripken became the Orioles manager, one of his first moves was to bring Billy up from the minor leagues. Cal would play shortstop, and Billy would play second base, just a few feet away. It was the first time in major-league history that a manager had two of his sons on the same team. It was also the first time that Cal and Billy had played on the same ball club since they were children.

The 1987 season was the first time a father managed two of his sons on a major-league team. From left to right are Billy Ripken, Cal Ripken, Sr., and Cal Ripken, Jr.

Cal loved being around his family. After all, how many other grown men get to visit the same cities, wear the same uniform, and go to work every day with their brother and dad? One of the toughest parts of being a pro athlete is that you are away from home so often while playing in other cities. It sure gets easier when some of your family travels with you.

Still, Mr. Ripken was careful not to give his sons any special treatment. He didn't want other players thinking that he favored his own sons. One of his rules was that, around the ballpark, the brothers did not call him "Dad" and he did not call them "Son." And when Billy went into a bad hitting slump during the 1987 season, Mr. Ripken benched him for a while, just as he would another player.

When they were boys, Cal and Billy competed against each other in everything. The brothers would play Ping-Pong for hours. They would shoot marbles until one owned all the other's best glassies. Sometimes they would just sit in their bedroom and take turns tossing a balled-up sock into a trash can. The point was not just to see which brother was better at something. It was also to keep practicing so they both could improve.

In baseball, however, Cal was always the better player. Billy, who is four years younger, never became a superstar. He was not a top hitter like his big brother. He almost never hit home runs. "Cal is a great player," Billy once said. "I just want people to call me a good player. I think I can do that if I follow Cal's advice. He told me that you've got to work your tail off all the time to make it in this game. You can't ever be satisfied." Billy would eventually play in the major leagues for 12 seasons. He led the Orioles in batting average in 1991.

But Billy was best at fielding. Like Cal, he is one of the smoothest glove men at his position. How come? Billy says it comes from years of having their dad hit ground balls to all the players during infield practice. "Dad always hit them harder to us than to anyone else," Billy says. "We had to learn to handle the tough ones."

They certainly learned well. In 1990 the two brothers set a major-league record for fewest errors, 11, by a shortstop-second baseman combination. Billy made just eight errors. Cal made just three. All those years of practicing together as kids seemed to pay off. Each brother always seemed to know where the other was going to be on every play.

In many ways, that 1987 season seemed perfect to Cal. He could stand on the field and look over at his brother playing second base. Meanwhile, his buddy, Eddie Murray, was playing first base. And his boss was his dad. What could be better?

While father and son were all business during the games, they were good friends afterward. Most nights they would stay at the ballpark until late at night. All the other players would have gone home. But Cal and his dad would stay to talk about at bats, plays, or pitchers. Or they would discuss just anything interesting that happened during that day's game.

In fact, Cal and his dad are such good friends that when Cal got married in 1987 Mr. Ripken was his best man. Billy was an usher at the wedding. Today, Cal and his wife, Kelly, have a daughter named Rachel and a son named Ryan.

In other ways, though, 1987 was not a good year for Cal or the rest of the Orioles. The team did not play any better for Mr. Ripken than it had under Earl Weaver. The Orioles won just 67 games while losing 95. Some of their players were injured. Some of their trades did not work out well. A few of their veteran players seemed to lose interest in the season.

Billy Ripken (right) stands by Cal's side while Cal is inducted into the Orioles hall of fame. Billy was not quite the player Cal was, but always supported his brother.

Sometimes, players on losing teams get down and stop giving their best. But Cal did not do that. As usual, he played every game, every inning. As usual, he hit 27 home runs and drove in 98 runs. His batting average was just .252, the worst since his first few games in 1981. But part of the reason for that was that opposing pitchers were no longer giving him good pitches to hit. They would rather pitch to his teammates.

Things did not get any better for the Orioles in 1988. In April, the team started the season by losing its first six games. It was clear that changes had to be made. The first change was a tough one. The team's owner and general manager removed Cal Ripken, Sr., as Orioles manager.

In baseball, as in all sports, managers and coaches get replaced whenever a team is playing poorly. The old joke is that the manager never really owns his job. Instead, he just borrows it for a while. Still, when Mr. Ripken left, it was heartbreaking for Cal and Billy. They had seen their lifelong dream come true. Now, after little more than one year, it was ending. Cal understood that these things happen in baseball. And he knew that his job was to keep going out every day and giving his best effort. Still, it was tough. At the time, Cal said, "I just have to block my personal feelings out of my mind. I just have to keep playing to win. I have to act like a professional."

Mr. Ripken stayed with the Orioles, returning to his old job as third-base coach. The new manager was Frank Robinson, a Hall-of-Fame outfielder who had starred for Baltimore in the 1960s. Robinson said his goal was to quickly turn the club around.

However, that was easier said than done. The Orioles lost their first game under Robinson, dropping them to 0-7 for the season. Then they lost their next game, and the next. By the middle of April, they had won none and lost 12. Now they were about to leave Baltimore for a two-week road trip. One more loss would tie an eighty-four-year-old record for the worst start ever by a major-league team.

Ripken wanted no part of this kind of record. Before the first road game against the Milwaukee Brewers, Ripken and Robinson called the Orioles together for a meeting. What could they do to win, they asked the players. No one had an answer. Certainly, they had all been trying hard. But maybe, everyone agreed, they could try a little harder.

It didn't help. The Orioles lost game 13, and then another, and then another. By the end of April, they had lost 21 straight games. It seemed to some that they might never win again.

On April 29, 1988, they finally won. Eddie Murray hit a first-inning homer. Cal had four hits and scored three runs. The Orioles beat the Chicago White Sox, 9-0, to end the worst stretch of baseball in the history of Major League Baseball.

After the season, a writer asked Ripken how bad he had felt during the losing streak.

"Nothing can be worse than this," Cal said. "But we can learn from this. No matter what happens in the future, we can say, 'We'll handle this. It can't be as bad as what happened in 1988.' We will all be stronger for it."

The Orioles won just 55 games and lost 107 in 1988. They finished in last place. Some fans worried that Cal would tire of

Orioles legend Frank Robinson replaced Cal, Sr., as Baltimore's manager during the 1988 season. Cal is arguing an umpire's call while Robinson stands by his player.

being a great player on a bad team. They wondered if he would leave the club to sign with another club when his contract was finished.

But Ripken had no such ideas. From the time he had been a little boy, the only team he wanted to play for was the Orioles. And like his hero, Brooks Robinson, he wanted to spend his entire career with one team. So in July 1988, not long after his father was replaced as manager, Ripken signed a new contract with the Orioles. It was a magnificent deal at that time. Cal would earn $2.45 million a year for three seasons. Suddenly, he was one of the best-paid players in all of sports. That only seemed fair, since he was one of the top athletes around.

The money was great, Cal said. But staying in Baltimore was the most important thing. After the Orioles' terrible season, he wanted to be there when the team turned things around. Cal told reporters, "I started a job when I came here in 1981. The job is far from being finished. So I'm staying in Baltimore. I've got work to do."

Mr. Dependable

Imagine not missing a day of school in ten years. Imagine having a job and not calling in sick for 1,735 days in a row. It seems impossible. After all, everyone gets the flu once in a while. Everyone who works needs an occasional day off to rest or play. Everyone that is, except Cal Ripken. For every day of the baseball season from May 30, 1982 until September 20, 1996, Ripken's name had been written into the Orioles starting lineup. When Cal decided to bench himself for the game on September 20, 1996, he had already shattered Lou Gehrig's record for consecutive games played. Ripken now owns the record at 2,632 games. In fact, at one point, Cal played every inning of

Even after the Orioles struggled mightily during the 1988 season, Ripken never lost his love for the game. That included making time for the fans.

every game for almost six full years. This is the MLB record for consecutive innings played, at 8,243. Of all Cal's deeds, some people think "The Streak" is his greatest accomplishment.

Sure, baseball is fun. But for the men who play it for a living it is also hard work. Players can get hurt by sliding, getting hit by a pitch, or just by running. Even those who don't get injured find themselves too tired to play on occasion. Or they may need to rest their minds to refocus.

But Cal Ripken was not like other players. One of his teammates, first baseman Randy Milligan, said, "Every player has days when he's not feeling so good. I have them all the time. But I've never heard Cal say he doesn't feel well. All he ever says is, 'I'm ready. When does the game start?'"

Only once in his first ten years did Ripken come close to missing a game. It happened on the second day of the 1985 season, against the Texas Rangers. Ripken, running the bases, got the spikes of his shoes stuck on second base. As he tried to lift his foot, his ankle twisted and he fell down. His ankle swelled up like a balloon.

The Orioles had the next day off so Cal stayed in bed. The following afternoon, no one expected him to play. But there he was taking batting practice before the game. He winced in pain as he swung the bat. But he played anyway. "I want to be in the thick of things," Cal said. "I always want to play. I never want to watch." Until Cal came along, baseball experts said Gehrig's mark was one that would never be topped. In fact, Gehrig earned the nickname The Iron Horse by playing so many games in a row. Even before Cal broke Gehrig's record, he had earned himself the nickname "The Iron Man." Many sports experts now say that Ripken's record is one that will likely stand forever.

One reason is that Ripken never got tired of baseball. He never stopped trying to get better. Johnny Oates, who managed the Orioles in 1991, said that Cal had not even missed infield practice or batting practice in ten years. One time in 1991, after going without a hit for two games, Cal came to the ballpark two hours early for extra hitting practice.

That kind of desire impressed his teammates. Cal knew that the only way to keep his streak going and remain one of baseball's top stars was to keep working and exercising. He used to wear a T-shirt in the clubhouse that said, "Fat Birds Don't Fly." It means that Orioles who don't stay in shape are not going to succeed.

Every day, Ripken did his sit-ups, push-ups, and pull-ups. In the winter, when there was no baseball, he played pick-up basketball games or swam a hundred laps across a pool. Instead of tiring him out, the extra work built up his strength.

After the Orioles disastrous 1988 season, the club made many changes. One was trading first baseman Eddie Murray, Cal's friend and the team's only other slugger. Manager Frank Robinson decided to bring up young players from the minors to see how they would do. No one expected much. But the 1989 Orioles played surprisingly well. They won 87 games, lost 75, and finished second in the AL East. Ripken, as usual, was the key player. And now, at age twenty-nine, he was one of the veteran leaders on the club.

Mostly, Cal always led by example. Off the field, he never

ripped the manager or umpires. He didn't complain about his salary. He didn't treat people rudely.

On the field, Cal made the most of his talent. He wasn't as fast as Rickey Henderson. He didn't have Jose Canseco's power swing, or Shawon Dunston's great arm. Nor did he have Ozzie Smith's ability to get to the ball. "He just finds ways to beat the other guy," said Frank Robinson. "When the game is on the line, he finds the way to win. Part of it is that he's so smart and studies the game so hard."

How smart? Here's one example. Late in the 1989 season, Robinson decided to put in rookie pitcher Ben McDonald for the first time. McDonald entered in the middle of the game, and he was nervous. There were runners on first and third base and a dangerous hitter at the plate. What a tough way for a rookie to break in!

Ripken, sensing how scared the young pitcher was, called timeout and trotted to the mound to calm him down. Cal had seen McDonald pitch in the minors. He knew that McDonald had been called for several balks. So Cal reminded McDonald to come to a complete stop. Then he said, "Just throw strikes, Ben. If they hit the ball, we'll get the outs for you. That's what we're here for."

McDonald's first pitch was over the plate. The batter, Cory Snyder, hit a slow two-hopper back up the middle. Ripken had studied Snyder before and knew where he usually hit the ball. So Cal was standing exactly in the right spot. He caught the ball easily and flipped it to his brother at second base to start a double play. McDonald had thrown his first major-league pitch and gotten two men out thanks to Ripken.

Because Cal was such an excellent hitter, people sometimes didn't notice his fielding. But he was one of the best. He had led the American League more than twenty times in different defensive categories. Back in 1984, he had set the league record by throwing out 584 runners. But in 1990 he set an even more impressive mark. In 161 games, he made just three errors. That broke the old record of six. Imagine handling 680 chances for the season and bobbling just three! The only other person to accomplish this feat was Omar Vizquel of the Cleveland Indians in 2000.

Cal was not as flashy a fielder as some of baseball's other top shortstops. With his big size, he couldn't dive around as quickly as they do. Instead, he played a style that is best described as "steady." He has big, soft hands that have been trained not to bobble balls. And, as the episode with Ben McDonald shows, he knows where to play the hitters. All those years of growing up around the clubhouse helped him learn the importance of that knowledge.

"The first rule of baseball is to catch the ball," Ripken says. "Then you have to know what to do with it after you catch it. A shortstop has to be prepared. You have to know the hitters. How do they hit with two strikes? How they hit with two balls? How do they adjust to each pitcher?"

That's a lot to learn. And it can only be learned by playing baseball and studying it day after day, year after year. And, certainly, Cal Ripken did that.

Ripken's fielding was an often overlooked part of his game. While he didn't have the range of some shortstops, he made up for it with sure hands and an accurate throwing arm.

Other than catcher, shortstop is baseball's most demanding position. The shortstop must be able to field hot grounders. He must have an arm strong enough to throw out runners from deep in the hole. And he must be quick enough to pivot, leap, and throw on the double play. For those reasons, it is also the most exhausting position.

Therefore, it is more amazing that Ripken had not missed a game in over 14 seasons. But by the middle of 1989, some fans and teammates began to wonder: Was Cal hurting his game by playing every day?

The questions began when Cal's batting statistics began to go down. Early in his career, he regularly batted over .300. But in 1989, he hit just .257. His home run totals also dropped from 27 in 1987, to 23 in 1988, to what was then a career-low 21 in 1989.

Ripken said the problem was that he was trying too hard. After Murray's trade, Cal was the Orioles' only slugger. So he was attempting to do it all himself. He stopped taking walks and began to swing at more bad pitches. The result was more outs. The solution, Ripken said, was to go back to his old batting style.

But others viewed it differently. Many said he looked tired. They said the demand of playing every game had taken too much out of him. They suggested that he take a rest.

Cal refused. "It used to bother me when people said I was hurting myself and hurting the team by playing every day," he said. "But I know I'm not. The least I can do is come out and play every day." Still, Cal knew inside that his hitting was getting worse. He realized it was time to make changes. After ten years of taking batting advice only from his father, Cal decided to seek someone else's opinion. Midway through the 1990 season, with his batting average down at .209, Cal went to Frank Robinson for help. This was a wise choice. Robinson is a Hall of Famer and one of the top home-run hitters in baseball history.

Robinson told Cal how he once went 22 at bats without a hit. Even the best ballplayers go through slumps, he said. After talking it over, the two men worked together in the batting cage. They came up with a new batting stance for Cal and a new approach. He would no longer chase bad pitches.

Cal's hitting improved immediately. His batting average rose to .250 by the end of the season. It was the lowest average of his career, but a lot better than the .209 he had been hitting earlier. After nine full seasons in the majors, Cal found himself looking forward to 1991 with the eagerness of a rookie. With his new approach, he predicted he would play as well as he had in his younger days.

Cal was wrong. He played a lot better.

Chapter 6

Hall of Fame Finish

During the winter before the 1991 season, Ripken and Robinson continued to tinker with Cal's batting style. Cal built a batting cage with a mechanical pitcher in his backyard so that he could practice every day. Here was a thirty-year-old veteran working with the dedication of a nineteen-year-old prospect.

Why? Because Cal could not stand having people regard him as less than one of the best in the business. He had read the stories suggesting that he was past his prime. He heard fans argue that he was tiring himself out by playing every game. Now, Cal wanted to show everyone, including himself, that he was still an all-star. "I looked in the mirror and asked, 'Is my talent dwindling?'" Cal

Ripken's performance during the 1990 season was not up to his standards. He worked on his swing during the off-season and had his best year in 1991.

said. "I had to get rid of the doubts. So I did two things before the 1991 season. I worked harder over the winter than I ever had before. And I mentally focused on what it would take to have a great season. That was my plan."

The plan worked. In spring training, one line drive after another flew off of Ripken's bat under the hot Florida sun. And the pounding continued when the regular season started.

In the fourth game of the year, against the Texas Rangers, Cal smacked a triple, a single, and a homer in his first four at bats. He came up in the eighth inning needing a double to hit for the cycle, which means getting each type of hit in a game. It didn't happen. Rangers pitcher Brad Arnsberg tried to sneak a fastball past Ripken, who sent his second home run of the game sailing over the center-field wall. For the night, Cal was four-for-five, with three runs scored and a career-best seven RBIs.

It was a great night, even for Cal. But the rest of the season wasn't too much different. A year after many people thought Cal had fallen from great to just good, he had the best season of his career. He hit .323 with 46 doubles, 34 homers, and 114 RBIs. He became the first shortstop to lead his league in every fielding category: putouts, assists, chances, double plays, and fielding percentage. He won the first Gold Glove Award of his career, meaning that opposing managers felt he was the American League's best-fielding shortstop.

Not only was this the best season of Cal's career, but it was also one of the greatest all-around seasons by any shortstop in baseball history. His 34 homers made him just the fourth shortstop ever to hit more than 30 in a year. In fact, he became only the second shortstop ever to bat over .300 with 30 homers and 100 RBIs in a season. Ernie Banks of the Chicago Cubs was the first.

The numbers tell just part of the story. They don't say anything about leadership. They don't explain how important Ripken's clutch hitting was to the Orioles.

Consider, for example, a game against the Seattle Mariners in late July 1991. It turned out to be Cal's 1,500th straight game, which earned him a standing ovation from the Baltimore crowd. It also was the night Cal was handed his trophy as the MVP of the 1991 All-Star game. That started another ovation.

The honors were nice. But honors don't win games. Ripken would have to do that himself. With the Orioles down 1-0 in the seventh inning, Cal came up with a runner on first. He quickly knocked Mariners hurler Rich DeLucia's first pitch out of the park for a home run. It won the game for the Orioles and earned Ripken his third standing ovation of the night.

"Without a doubt, this was a special night," Ripken said afterward. "I try to downplay it and not get caught up in it, but the way the fans received me, I hold this night deep."

Cal never needs to worry about how the fans feel about him. He was easily the most popular player in Baltimore and one of the most popular in baseball. His performance was one reason. The way he treats people was another.

Ripken and his wife Kelly helped start a program in Baltimore to teach reading to adults. They have given hundreds of thousands of dollars to the program.

In addition, Cal spent one afternoon a week at Baltimore's stadium answering every letter he received from fans. He had been known to hang around the ballpark for more than an hour after games, signing more than five hundred autographs.

"That part goes with the job," he said. "If no one wanted to talk to you, I guess that would mean you're having a pretty bad season." It wasn't just fans who recognized Ripken's great 1991 season. So did the baseball writers who vote for the league's MVP award. That November, they decided that Cal was the AL's top player for the second time in his career. He received fifteen of the twenty-four first-place votes. Finishing second was the Detroit Tigers' Cecil Fielder, who had pounded out a league-best 44 home runs.

In winning the award, Ripken became the first player from a losing team to be named MVP. Despite Cal's phenomenal performance, the Orioles finished in sixth place in 1991. So it was all a mixed blessing for Ripken.

"When you're an athlete in a team sport, the only thing that really matters is winning," Ripken said after being handed the gold MVP trophy. "I appreciate this honor, but nothing beats playing in the World Series. I would trade this award for another chance to be there."

Did Ripken get another chance to play in the World Series? Baseball teams can go from bad to good in one season these days. And the Orioles certainly had some good young players. But most major leaguers consider themselves lucky to be on one championship team. Ripken wanted two.

A few days after winning the 1991 MVP award, Ripken went to a party honoring him at the Orioles' brand-new stadium. He drank milk from a champagne glass. He toasted not himself, but

On September 6, 1995, Cal Ripken, Jr., broke Lou Gehrig's record for most consecutive games played. It is a record many feel will never again be broken.

his teammates. He told them how he had worried just a year earlier that his career was headed downward. His return to greatness, he said, could be the start of the Orioles' return to greatness.

The Orioles did contend in 1992, and Ripken was again a key part of their success. Late in the season, he signed a five-year, $32.5 million contract that made him the best-paid player in baseball history at that time. By the time the contract ended, Ripken became regarded as not just a future Hall of Famer, but as one of the best players ever.

By the end of his career, Cal had broken Ernie Banks's record for most homers by a shortstop. He only needed about 20 more for that record entering the 1993 season and continued to play until after the 2001 season. He finished his career with an astonishing 431.

During the 1997 season, Cal switched from shortstop to third base for the rest of his career. He would even star for the American League All-Star team later in the year and for the next two seasons at third base. In 1998, Ripken broke Joe Cronin's record of 1,424 runs batted in by an AL player who spent most of his career as a shortstop. Ripken finished his career with 1,695. Cronin was regarded by most baseball experts as the best shortstop ever in the American League. That opinion has since changed.

Ripken decided he would retire after the 2001 season. He made his final appearance as an all-star for the American League team at Safeco Field in Seattle. Alex Rodriguez was the starting shortstop, but he insisted that he switch positions with Cal for the first inning. This way, Cal could play shortstop one

The 2001 season was Ripken's last as a player. He was honored when shortstop Alex Rodriguez switched positions with Cal to let Ripken play shortstop during the first inning of that year's All-Star game. Ripken hit a home run and was named All-Star Game MVP in his final All-Star game appearance.

last time in the All-Star game. Ripken hit a solo home run in the third inning, and earned his second All-Star Game MVP award.

Of course, by the time he finished, Ripken had broken Lou Gehrig's record for playing in the most games in a row. It is a record that may stand forever. That would be his greatest achievement, especially considering that he played the exhausting position of shortstop. In a way, Ripken has done for shortstop what basketball great Magic Johnson did for the position of point guard. He proved that a six-foot, four-inch, 220-pounder can play the position requiring the most grace, quickness, and agility. Ripken once said that he wanted to be remembered as an "iron man," meaning a player who went out there and put it on the line every day. He wanted people to say, "They couldn't keep Cal out of the lineup." And he wanted to be recalled as a winning player.

He was inducted into the National Baseball Hall of Fame in 2007. In his acceptance speech, Ripken talked about how he always sought to use his fame to inspire others. He said:

> It took me a little while, but I did come to realize that baseball was just one part of my life with the possible exception of this weekend, of course. This was never more clear to me than when we had children. I realized that the secret of life is life, and a bigger picture came into focus. Games were and are important, but people and how you impact on them are most important. While we all work to develop into productive people for our own happiness, it is also vital that we do so for the good of society as a whole.

Since retiring from baseball, Ripken has remained very active. His first big project was starting Ripken Baseball, Inc. The organization is dedicated to helping spread baseball around the world. Cal has also bought three minor-league baseball teams: The Aberdeen Ironbirds (affiliated with the Baltimore Orioles), the Augusta Green Jackets (affiliated with the San Francisco Giants), and the Charlotte Stone Crabs (affiliated with the Tampa Bay Rays). He also has the Cal Ripken baseball

NATIONAL

★ ★ ★

BASEBALL

Cal Ripken, Jr., was inducted
into the National Baseball Hall
of Fame on July 29, 2007.

HA   ME

NATIONAL
BASEBALL
HALL OF FAME

NATIONAL
BASEBALL
HALL OF FAME

league, a collegiate-level baseball organization that uses only wooden bats.

Ripken once said, "I have talent, no doubt. My advantage is that I know the game well. The reason is that I grew up in it and had a good teacher in my father. I'm sure that whatever I am as a man and as a ballplayer comes from the way I was raised."

"But am I a superstar? Oh, no. I don't think I stack up with the great players in the league."

Anyone who has seen Cal Ripken, Jr., play knows differently.

Career Statistics

Year	Team	G	AB	Runs	Hits	2B	3B	HR	RBI	SB	AVG
1981	Orioles	23	39	1	5	0	0	0	0	0	.128
1982	Orioles	160	598	90	158	32	5	28	93	3	.264
1983	Orioles	162	663	121	211	47	2	27	102	0	.318
1984	Orioles	162	641	103	195	37	7	27	86	2	.304
1985	Orioles	161	642	116	181	32	5	26	110	2	.282
1986	Orioles	162	627	98	177	35	1	25	81	4	.282
1987	Orioles	162	624	97	157	28	3	27	98	3	.252
1988	Orioles	161	575	87	152	25	1	23	81	2	.264
1989	Orioles	162	646	80	166	30	0	21	93	3	.257
1990	Orioles	161	600	78	150	28	4	21	84	3	.250
1991	Orioles	162	650	99	210	46	5	34	114	6	.323
1992	Orioles	162	637	73	160	29	1	14	72	4	.251
1993	Orioles	162	641	87	165	26	3	24	90	1	.257
1994	Orioles	112	444	71	140	19	3	13	75	1	.315
1995	Orioles	144	550	71	144	33	2	17	88	0	.262
1996	Orioles	163	640	94	178	40	1	26	102	1	.278
1997	Orioles	162	615	79	166	30	0	17	84	1	.270
1998	Orioles	161	601	65	163	27	1	14	61	0	.271
1999	Orioles	86	332	51	113	27	0	18	57	0	.340
2000	Orioles	83	309	43	79	16	0	15	56	0	.256
2001	Orioles	128	477	43	114	16	0	14	68	0	.239
Career Totals		3,001	11,551	1,647	3,184	603	44	431	1,695	36	.276

G = Games
AB = At Bats
2B = Doubles
3B = Triples

HR = Home Runs
RBI = Runs Batted In
SB = Stolen Bases
AVG = Batting Average

Where to Write

Where to Write Cal Ripken, Jr.

Cal Ripken
c/o Ripken Baseball
1427 Clarkview Rd
Suite 100
Baltimore, MD 21209
USA

Facebook:

http://www.facebook.com/pages/Cal-Ripken-Jr/19523855
3838824

On the internet at:

http://www.baseball-reference.com/players/r/ripkeca01.shtml

http://www.ripkenbaseball.com/calripken/bio/

Index